2022
SAN DIEGO

The Restaurant Enthusiast's Discriminating Guide

Andrew Delaplaine

Andrew Delaplaine is the Food Enthusiast.
When he's not playing tennis,
he dines anonymously
at the Publisher's (often considerable) expense.

Senior Editor – James Cubby

SAN DIEGO

The Restaurant Enthusiast's
Discriminating Guide

Table of Contents

Introduction

San Diego is a great place for a vacation because it's filled with adventures. Located on the Pacific Ocean in Southern California, San Diego is the second largest city in the state but has small town appeal. Sure there are plenty of beaches in San Diego but most people visit for the many theme parks like Sea World, Sea World Aquatic Waterpark, San Diego Wild Animal Park, and the world famous San Diego Zoo.

San Diego is heaven to surfers and beach enthusiasts. San Diego beaches are incredible and one of the main beaches is Mission Beach, located off Highway 8 West. There you will find the Historic Belmont Park, like a Coney Island west, where you'll find a roller coaster, bumper cars, a family arcade, and a variety of food vendors. Mission Beach is a favorite of surfers and many San Diegans can be spotted surfing every day, rain or shine because of the wealth of gentle surf breaks and year-round waves.

Shopping is an Olympic sport in San Diego with so many shopping centers, regular malls, and outlet malls. San Diego's biggest mall is Fashion Valley Mall, 1.7 million square feet of shopping, which houses major names like Neiman Marcus, Nordstrom, Macy's, Bloomingdales, Gucci, Guess, Hugo Boss, J.Crew, Louis Vuitton, Ted Baker, Old Navy, H&M, Tiffany's & Co., and Hugo Boss. Fashion Valley is the largest mall in San Diego and one of the largest in California. If outlet shopping is your bag, then you'll love the wealth of outlet centers on the outskirts of San Diego with shops like BCBG Max Azria, Kenneth Cole, Michael Kors, Tommy Hilfiger, and Polo Ralph Lauren.

San Diego is filled with theme parks, museums, and interesting attractions. Here are some that can't be missed. SeaWorld Aquatica Waterpark, a fairly new offering, combines the excitement of a water park

filled with thrilling rides and the wonder of Sea World. Balboa Park, a group of museums, parks, gardens and arboretums, offers a maze of flowering gardens with neo-classical Spanish architecture and a beautiful clock tower. The world famous San Diego Zoo, located in Balboa Park, is probably the premier zoo of North America with over 100 acres of displays and habitats. Sea World, probably best known as the home of Shamu, has a wonderful showcase of interactive exhibits featuring aquatic animals. Birch Aquarium features an impressive selection of exhibits that include physical oceanography, standard aquarium fish and a massive kelp tank. Point Loma Lighthouse allows visitors an incredible panoramic view of the Naval Air Station, downtown San Diego, the Coronado Bridge and even a glimpse of the

distant mountains. Historic Old Town San Diego, known as the Birthplace of California, offers a walking tour through history with a variety of attractions including a professional theatre, museums, sartisans, galleries and shops. San Diego Maritime Museum, located in the San Diego Bay on the west side of North Harbor Drive, houses one of the largest collections of historic sea vessels in the U.S. including the world's oldest active sailing ship. The USS Midway Museum, downtown on North Harbor Drive, offers an unforgettable sea adventure with over 60 exhibits and 29 restored aircraft.

Adventures abound in San Diego and with such great weather all year long it's a natuaral mecca for those who love the outdoors. Sailing is one of the favorite pastimes for visitors and locals alike with Mission Bay and San Diego Bay providing ideal spots for sailing, windsurfing and jet skiing. San Diego, known for its sailors, offers many sailing opportunities with the number of marinas available for boaters. Opportunities for water sports are endless in San Diego and scuba diving is popular year-round with dives offering a peek at underwater kelp beds and other sea life. Kayaking is another favorite activity as San Diego has great spots to kayak like Mission Bay, Sunset Beach, Kearny Mesa, Ocean side and La Jolla. Those interested in whale-watching, another favorite pastime as California gray whales migrate south along the cost during February, should try the overlook in Cabrillo National Monument in Point Loma. For the daring or those who wish to see the

ocean from above, try hang gliding off the cliffs above the Pacific Ocean (training and tandem glides with an expert are available). Another unique adventure popular in San Diego is rock climbing, best practiced outdoors but the novice should try one of the many indoor facilities before venturing to the cliffs. Golfers will be please to discover that there are many public and private golf courses in San Diego and the Torrey Pines Golf Course in nearby La Jolla hosts the PGA Tour Buick Invitational annually.

San Diego, like any large city, has a multitude of restaurants from fine dining to fast food. The city also has a thriving microbrewery scene with 44 breweries and growing. Many of the breweries are intimate micro or nanobreweries but some house large restaurants.

The A to Z Listings

Ridiculously Extravagant
Sensible Alternatives
Quality Bargain Spots

ADDISON AT THE GRAND DEL MAR
5200 Grand del Mar Way, San Diego, 858-314-1900
www.addisondelmar.com

CUISINE: French
DRINKS: Full bar
SERVING: Dinner; closed Sun & Mon
PRICE RANGE: $$$$
Upscale French eatery (this place will remind you of
an experience at a Thomas Keller eatery) with two set
menus: Chef's Tasting menu and a Four Course
menu. Menu favorite: Mushroom Lasagna. The
emphasis on seasonal dishes based on what's
available is pure Keller. Delicious bread courses and
creative dessert – whipped yogurt over iced citrus
amuse bouche.

AMERICANA RESTAURANT
1454 Camino Del Mar, (Between 14th St & 15th St),
Del Mar, 858-794-6838
www.americanarestaurant.com
CUISINE: American
DRINKS: Full Bar
SERVING: Breakfast, Lunch & Dinner
PRICE RANGE: $$
NEIGHBORHOOD: Del Mar
A local's favorite, this popular eatery offers a creative
menu of American cuisine. Menu favorites include:
Blackened Salmon and Grilled Baby Lamb Chops.
The menu also features seven desserts and six dessert
wines, all worth tasting, especially the Caramelized
Banana Tarte Tatin, served with warm dulce de leche
ice cream almond brittle.

A.R. VALENTIEN
11480 N Torrey Pines Rd, La Jolla, 858-777-6635
www.lodgetorreypines.com/dine

CUISINE: American (New)
DRINKS: Full bar
SERVING: Breakfast/Lunch/Dinner
PRICE RANGE: $$$$
Located at the **Lodge at Torrey Pines**, this upscale eatery serves artisanal dishes like Duck Confit and Hanger Steak. Beautiful view. Nice wine pairings. Great place for a very special occasion.

AQUI ES TEXCOCO
520 Broadway, Chula Vista, 619-427-4045
www.aquiestexcoco.com
CUISINE: Mexican
DRINKS: Beer & Wine
SERVING: Breakfast/Lunch/Dinner
PRICE RANGE: $
NEIGHBORHOOD: Chula Vista
Not your typical Mexican food joint, this casual eatery features traditional Barbacoa-style lamb – their

specialty. The menu includes lots of homemade sides and classic Mexican desserts.

BAHIA DON BRAVO
5504 La Jolla Blvd (b/t Forward St & Midway St), La Jolla, 858-454-8940
www.donbravogrill.com **WEBSITE DOWN AT PRESSTIME**
CUISINE: Mexican
DRINKS: Beer & Wine
SERVING: Breakfast, Lunch, & Dinner
PRICE RANGE: $
NEIGHBORHOOD: La Jolla
Popular eatery offering standard Mexican fare – everything from fish and chicken burritos, lobster tacos to fajitas. Daily specials. Grab a warm churro for dessert.

BENCOTTO ITALIAN KITCHEN
750 W Fir St, San Diego, 619-450-4786
www.lovebencotto.com
CUISINE: Italian
DRINKS: Full bar
SERVING: Lunch/Dinner; Dinner only on Monday
PRICE RANGE: $$
NEIGHBORHOOD: Little Italy
Chic bi-level eatery featuring a menu of artisanal Italian eats, including lots of pasta and seafood dishes. Nice selection of dishes to share. Menu pick: Spinach and ricotta ravioli.
& classic desserts. Impressive list of Italian desserts.

BETTER BUZZ COFFEE ROASTERS

801 University Ave, San Diego, 619-269-2740
www.betterbuzzcoffee.com
CUISINE: Coffee & Tea
DRINKS: No Booze
SERVING: 5:30 a.m. – 7 p.m.
PRICE RANGE: $$
NEIGHBORHOOD: Hancock Park
Coffee spot that serves and sells a variety of coffees
and coffee products. This place also offers a menu of
snacks, sandwiches, and Acai bowls. Great selection
of signature drinks.

BIG KITCHEN CAFÉ

3003 Grape St (between 30th St & Fern St), San Diego, 619-234-5789

www.judysbigkitchen.com

CUISINE: American/Breakfast

DRINKS: No Booze

SERVING: Breakfast & Brunch (closes around 2 p.m.)

PRICE RANGE: $$

NEIGHBORHOOD: Golden Hill/South Park

This popular breakfast spot makes the first meal of the day a treat. Most of the veggies are fresh (except the spinach—they don't like to wash it). The breads are all homemade, as well: from the muffins to the coffee cakes. The turkey breast is a fresh roasted on the premises, and they honey bake their own hams. This place—as simple and charming as it is—also is a center for cultural events, including theatre, music, poetry and art. Menu favorites include: Turkey & eggs and Protein Pancake – a 12-inch pancake cooked to perfection.

BLIND LADY ALE HOUSE
3416 Adams Ave, San Diego, 619-255-2491
www.blindladyalehouse.com
CUISINE: Pizza
DRINKS: Full bar
SERVING: Dinner, Lunch Fri - Sun
PRICE RANGE: $$
NEIGHBORHOOD: Normal Heights

Tavern-style eatery featuring communal tables. Great selection of wood-fired pizzas. Impressive list of craft beers. Casual atmosphere complete with TVs for watching the games.

BUONA FORCHETTA
3001 Beech St, San Diego, 619-381-4844
www.buonaforchettasd.com
CUISINE: Pizza/Italian
DRINKS: Full bar
SERVING: Lunch/Dinner, Dinner only Mon & Tues
PRICE RANGE: $$
NEIGHBORHOOD: South Park
Popular pizzeria featuring wood-fired pies, fresh pasta and global wines. Menu picks: Pizelle, artichokes and pizza in a jar. Great pastas. If you've saved room for dessert, try the fried pizza dough with Nutella. Usually a wait for tables.

CAFFE CALABRIA
3933 30th St, (Between University Ave & Lincoln Ave), San Diego, 619-683-7787

www.caffecalabria.com
CUISINE: Pizza
DRINKS: Beer & Wine Only
SERVING: Lunch & Dinner
PRICE RANGE: $
NEIGHBORHOOD: North Park
This Italian–style coffeehouse serves some of the best coffee in town as well as a menu that features pizza made from the wood-burning pizza oven. Nice variety of pizzas including vegetarian and gluten-free. This building used to be a Bank of America branch, and you can still see the vault.

CAMPFIRE
2725 State St, Carlsbad, 760-637-5121

https://www.thisiscampfire.com
CUISINE: American (New)
DRINKS: Full Bar
SERVING: Dinner; Closed Tues
PRICE RANGE: $$$
NEIGHBORHOOD: Beech Ave & Christiansen Way
Popular eatery offering a creative menu of wood-fired American cuisine. And let me make this clear—the wood-fired angle affects every aspect of this cozy place oozing with charm, from the smoked and grilled meats, seafood and veggies, to some of their cocktails. Favorites: Grilled tiger prawns and Roasted Lamb head. Indoor/outdoor seating. This place is intimate enough for a date night, but just as suitable as a family dining place.

CANTINA MAYAHUEL

2934 Adams Ave, San Diego, 619-283-6292
https://cantinamayahuelsd.com/
CUISINE: Mexican
DRINKS: Full bar
SERVING: Lunch/Dinner, Dinner only Sun & Mon
PRICE RANGE: $$
NEIGHBORHOOD: University Heights
Popular low-key eatery offering authentic Mexican fare like Mole dishes and fish tacos. Great tortilla chips. Tasty margaritas.

CARNITAS' SNACK SHACK

100 Park Blvd, San Diego, 619-294-7675
www.carnitassnackshack.com
CUISINE: American
DRINKS: No Booze
SERVING: Lunch & Dinner, open daily
PRICE RANGE: $$

NEIGHBORHOOD: Petco Park
This infamous counter-service eatery is known for its limited menu (only 10 items are on the menu) but pork is the focus: pork sandwiches, farm-fresh food, and local craft beer. When I say "pork sandwich," what I mean is pulled pork, pork schnitzel, pickled pepperoncini relish, bacon and the aioli they make right here on site. Other menu winners include the tasty Carnitas Tacos. Chefs from other joints come here late at night when they get off. Large portions. Outdoor seating.

CATANIA
7863 Girard Ave, La Jolla, 858-551-5105
www.cataniasd.com
CUISINE: Italian
DRINKS: Full bar
SERVING: Lunch/Dinner
PRICE RANGE: $$$

Perched atop La Plaza Center, this popular eatery specializes in wood-fired pizzas, pasta, and creative dishes. A big emphasis on seafood expertly prepared. You can see the palm trees down by the ocean. Menu picks: Squid Ink Pasta and Fungi Pizza. Creative desserts.

CORI PASTIFICIO TRATTORIA
2977 Upas St, San Diego, 619-573-6159
https://www.coripasta.com
CUISINE: Italian
DRINKS: Beer & Wine
SERVING: Dinner; Closed Mon
PRICE RANGE: $$
NEIGHBORHOOD: North Park
Italian Trattoria featuring a creative menu of classics. (The chef is Sicilian.) Favorites: Lamb chops and Eggplant Parmesan. Menu changes often. Vegan Options. Reservations recommended.

COWBOY STAR
640 10th Ave (between G St & Market St), San
Diego, 619-450-5880
www.thecowboystar.com
CUISINE: Steakhouse, American
DRINKS: Full Bar
SERVING: Dinner nightly, Lunch weekdays
PRICE RANGE: $$$
NEIGHBORHOOD: Downtown / Gaslamp
With a rustic-chic décor, this steakhouse (they have
their own on-site butcher shop) serves a menu of
standard meat with a few selections of ofal and wild
game. The atmosphere is so opposite of what you've
come to expect from steakhouses catering to the
expensive-account crowd. Here it's ultra casual and
fun. See if you can snag a steat at the chef's counter.
The menu features a variety of regional American
heirloom recipes. Menu favorites include: Roasted
Elk Rack and Pan Roasted Salmon. The impressive
wine list features mostly California labels.

THE CRACK SHACK
2266 Kettner Blvd (b/t Ivy St & Juniper St), San
Diego, 619-795-3299
www.crackshack.com
CUISINE: American (Traditional)
DRINKS: Full Bar
SERVING: Breakfast, Lunch, & Dinner
PRICE RANGE: $$
NEIGHBORHOOD: Little Italy
Known for their chicken and non-GMO egg dishes
and organic ingredients from local farms. Outdoor
patio. Order at the counter. Favorites: Chicken

sandwiches and Sea Senorita sandwich (made with seared rare tuna). Delicious thick ice cream shakes.

CUCINA URBANA
505 Laurel St, San Diego, 619-239-2222
www.urbankitchengroup.com/cucina-urbana-bankers-hill/
CUISINE: Italian/Pizza
DRINKS: Full bar
SERVING: Lunch/Dinner, Dinner only Sat - Mon
PRICE RANGE: $$
NEIGHBORHOOD: Downtown/Banker's Hill
Contemporary Italian eatery and wine shop. Nice menu of Italian fare and custom-made pizzas. Menu favorites: Grilled Octopus, ceci bean and dehydrated tomato pizza. Crafted cocktails. Reservations recommended.

DIJA MARA

232 S Coast Hwy, Oceanside, 760-231-5376
https://dijamara.com
CUISINE: Indonesian/American (New)
DRINKS: Beer & Wine
SERVING: Dinner, Lunch & Dinner on Sun; Closed
Mon
PRICE RANGE: $$
NEIGHBORHOOD: Michigan Ave & Pier View
Way
Popular industrial-chic eatery featuring a Balinese-
inspired menu. Favorites: Pork Belly Skewers and
Beef Tartare. Most dishes are meant to be shared.
Reservations recommended 2-3 weeks in advance.

Creative cocktails with names to match like Paloma and Gypsy King.

ET VOILÀ!
3015 Adams Ave, San Diego, 619-209-7759
https://etvoilabistro.com
CUISINE: French
DRINKS: Full Bar
SERVING: Dinner; Closed Mon
PRICE RANGE: $$$
NEIGHBORHOOD: University Heights, North Park

Neighborhood bistro bursting with charm featuring a menu of traditional French cuisine with a modern twist. Very cozy bar and the dining room is ultra-comfy. The souffles here are astounding. Favorites: Roasted duck breast in cherry sauce and Boeuf Bourguignon. Curated wine list.

FATHOM BISTRO, BAIT & TACKLE
1776 Shelter Island Dr, San Diego, 619-222-5835
www.fathombistro.com
CUISINE: American/Hot Dogs
DRINKS: Beer & Wine
SERVING: Dinner Tues – Fri, Lunch & Dinner Sat & Sun, closed Mon
PRICE RANGE: $
NEIGHBORHOOD: Point Loma
Located on the pier, this popular eatery offers a menu of homemade sausages and hot dogs. Limited brunch menu on the weekends. Nice selection of beers. Few tables – inside and out.

THE FISHERY
5040 Cass St (between Opal St & Loring St), San Diego, 858-272-9985
www.thefishery.com
CUISINE: Seafood
DRINKS: Beer & Wine Only
SERVING: Lunch & Dinner
PRICE RANGE: $$

NEIGHBORHOOD: Pacific Beach

Located inside a midcentury warehouse just oozing character and "atmosphere," this eatery offers a menu of seafood and sushi. There's also a seafood market. Menu favorites include the Macadamia Crusted Halibut and Albacore Belly, but while these are very appealing, I inevitably end up with the simply fabulous shrimp tacos—using Mexican shrimp,

tomatillo sauce, a coleslaw made of cilantro and of course salsa fresca. Wash these babies down with cold beer or a sharp dry white wine and you'll be glad you stopped in this elegant and at the same time homey winner.

FORT OAK

1011 Fort Stockton Dr, San Diego, 619-722-3398
https://www.fortoaksd.com
CUISINE: American (New)
DRINKS: Full Bar
SERVING: Dinner; Closed Tues
PRICE RANGE: $$$
NEIGHBORHOOD: Hawk St & Ibis St, Mission
Hills

Modern eatery offering American cuisine and wood-fired seafood. Hard to beat experience here with its upmarket dining room and wonderful bar area. Favorites: Boiled Oysters & Grilled Prawns and Duck Breast. Unique desserts.

GEORGE'S AT THE COVE
1250 Prospect St, La Jolla, 858-454-4244
www.georgesatthecove.com
CUISINE: American (New)
DRINKS: Full bar
SERVING: Lunch/Dinner
PRICE RANGE: $$$
Elegant eatery offering beautiful ocean views and a menu of Southwest California cuisine with a heavy focus on seafood. Here you have the choice of eating on the casual rooftop terrace, or the gastrobar where the focus is on craft cocktails, or the third option in the 3-floor space is the fine dining level. Whatever you choose, you're in for stunning ocean views. Menu picks: Spaghetti with Clams and Blackened Fish Sandwich. Nice menu of cocktails.

HERB & WOOD
2210 Kettner Blvd (b/t Ivy St & Juniper St), San Diego, 619-955-8495
www.herbandwood.com
CUISINE: American (New)/Pizza/Seafood
DRINKS: Full Bar
SERVING: Dinner; Lunch on Sun
PRICE RANGE: $$$
NEIGHBORHOOD: Little Italy

Locals' favorite serving rustic, wood-fired dishes. Favorites: Seared scallops and Tomahawk steak with lobster mushroom sauce. Old-school cocktails.

HODAD'S

5010 Newport Ave (between Broadway and 10th Ave), San Diego, 619-224-4623
www.hodadies.com
CUISINE: Burgers
DRINKS: Beer & Wine Only
SERVING: Lunch & Dinner

PRICE RANGE: $$
NEIGHBORHOOD: Ocean Beach
This retro inspired eatery offers guests an opportunity to dine inside restored cars. Menu favorites include: Guido Burger and the Classic Bacon Cheeseburger.

Other favorites include the Chicken Burger and the Veggieburger.

IRONSIDE FISH & OYSTER
1654 India St, San Diego, 619-269-3033
www.ironsidefishandoyster.com
CUISINE: Seafood/Raw Bar
DRINKS: Full bar
SERVING: Lunch/Dinner
PRICE RANGE: $$
NEIGHBORHOOD: Little Italy
Popular nautical designed eatery serving seafood dishes with a raw bar. Menu picks: Lobster roll and Sea Bass. Great cocktails.

JAKE'S
1660 Coast Blvd, Del Mar, 858-755-2002
www.jakesdelmar.com
CUISINE: American (New)/Seafood
DRINKS: Full Bar
SERVING: Lunch & Dinner; Only Dinner on Mon
PRICE RANGE: $$$

NEIGHBORHOOD: Del Mar
Great dining experience. Make a reservation if you want a table with an ocean view. Great selection of seafood. Delicious desserts.

JAYNE'S GASTROPUB
4677 30th St, San Diego, 619-563-1011
www.jaynesgastropub.com
CUISINE: Gastropub
DRINKS: Full bar
SERVING: Dinner; closed Sun
PRICE RANGE: $$
NEIGHBORHOOD: University Heights/North Park
Casual eatery featuring mainly modern British pub fare. Favorites: Meatballs and Duck breast with gnocchi. Great sticky toffee pudding. Great wine list. Tables inside and on the courtyard.

JEUNE ET JOLIE

2659 State St, Carlsbad, 760-637-5266
https://www.jeune-jolie.com
CUISINE: French
DRINKS: Full Bar
SERVING: Dinner; Closed Mon & Tues
PRICE RANGE: $$$$
NEIGHBORHOOD: Beech Ave & Christiansen Way
Upscale eatery offering a prix-fix menu of creative
French cuisine. The gorgeous open kitchen is a
wonder to look at. The menu is chic without being
Michelin star stuffy. The place became popular vas
soon as it opened and has maintained that level of
excitement. A la carte menu and wine pairing

available. Vegan options. Menu picks: Lamb tartare
and Rabbit.

JSIX RESTAURANT
616 J St, San Diego, 619-531-8744
www.jsixrestaurant.com
CUISINE: American (New)
DRINKS: Full bar
SERVING: Lunch/Dinner
PRICE RANGE: $$
NEIGHBORHOOD: East Village
Popular eatery with a menu that's primarily
California fare with a focus on seafood. Favorites:
Goat cheese salad and Scallop entrée. Creative
desserts. Reservations recommended.

JUNIPER & IVY
2228 Kettner Blvd (between Ivy St & Juniper St), San
Diego, 619-269-9036
www.juniperandivy.com
CUISINE: American
DRINKS: Full Bar
SERVING: Dinner, open daily
PRICE RANGE: $$$
NEIGHBORHOOD: Little Italy
This popular restaurant offers Top Chef Richard
Blais's creative menu of American cuisine served in
beautifully designed modern setting. Menu favorites
include: a delectable crab cake, Ensenada white sea
bass, Lamb Carpaccio and Ahi Tuna Tartare. Superior
craft cocktails and an excellent wine program. This
can be one of the tougher places to book, so reserve
well ahead.

K SANDWICHES

7604 Linda Vista Rd (at Mesa College Dr), San Diego, 858-384-7373
www.ksandwiches.com
CUISINE: Vietnamese, Sandwiches
DRINKS: No Booze
SERVING: Lunch & Dinner
PRICE RANGE: $$
NEIGHBORHOOD: Clairemont
Great selection of Vietnamese sandwiches. Very authentic. About the only switch is their use of crunchy French baguettes instead of the traditional bun, but I like it very much, and they're bigger than the normal Banh Mi sandwiches. Menu favorites include: Pork Meat Ball sandwich and the Banh Mi Xiu Mai. They also serve boba and smoothies.

KAITO SUSHI

130 N El Camino Real, Encinitas, 760-634-2746
www.kaitorestaurant.net
CUISINE: Japanese/Sushi

DRINKS: Full bar
SERVING: Dinner; closed Sun
PRICE RANGE: $$$
NEIGHBORHOOD: Encinitas
Sushi purists love this place because it has a menu of exotic raw dishes. Favorites: Red snapper Kama and Sashimi. Interesting selection of sake – no list, they just ask what type you like. (Though all sake tastes the same to me.)

KETTNER EXCHANGE
2001 Kettner Blvd, San Diego, 619-255-2001
www.kettnerexchange.com
CUISINE: American (Traditional)
DRINKS: Full bar
SERVING: Dinner, Lunch on Sat & Sun
PRICE RANGE: $$
NEIGHBORHOOD: Little Italy
Casual eatery offering a menu of creative American cuisine with a global flare. Great place for weekend brunch. Great burgers and Drunken noodles. Delicious selection of desserts. Reservations definitely recommended.

KINDRED
1503 30th St (b/t Beech St & Cedar St), San Diego, 619-546-9653
www.barkindred.com
CUISINE: American (Traditional)/Vegan
DRINKS: Full Bar
SERVING: Dinner, Lunch on Sat & Sun
PRICE RANGE: $$
NEIGHBORHOOD: Golden Hill, South Park

Modern eatery offering a great selection of vegan fare. Favorites: Wizard Bowl salad and Cauliflower Steak (of course it's not steak but its tasty). Note: Loud Heavy Metal music can be a bit overwhelming.

KONO'S SURF CLUB CAFÉ
704 Garnet Ave (between Mission Blvd & Ocean Blvd), San Diego, 858-230-7355
www.konoscafepb.com
CUISINE: Burgers/Breakfast
DRINKS: No Booze
SERVING: Lunch & Dinner
PRICE RANGE: $$
NEIGHBORHOOD: Pacific Beach

This is one of the locals' favorite breakfast spots and there's always a line at this oceanfront café. Menu favorites include: Breakfast Burrito and French toast. Cash only.

LAS CUATROS MILPAS

1857 Logan Ave (b/t Crosby St & Beardsley St), San Diego, 619-234-4460
www.las-cuatro-milpas.com
CUISINE: Mexican
DRINKS: No Booze
SERVING: Breakfast & Lunch; Closed Sun
PRICE RANGE: $
NEIGHBORHOOD: Barrio Logan
Basic Mexican eatery serving up homemade tortillas since 1933. Everything is made from scratch. They cook the stews for 12 hours. Dining on picnic tables. There's usually a line but it moves fast. CASH ONLY.

LITTLE ITALY MERCATO

600 W Date St, San Diego, 619-233-3901
https://sandiegomarkets.com/
NEIGHBORHOOD: Little Italy
Saturday market with over 150 vendors offering fresh produce, meat, eggs, crafts, plants, prepared foods, pastries, art, and much more. Great spot for breakfast. Many of the vendors offer free samples. Live music.

LYNDA SANDWICH

15380 Beach Blvd (between Bishop Ave & W McFadden Ave), Westminster, 714-942-0932
www.lyndasandwich.net

CUISINE: Sandwiches, Vietnamese
DRINKS: No Booze
SERVING: Lunch & Dinner
PRICE RANGE: $$
NEIGHBORHOOD: Westminster
This popular sandwich shop is owned by the
Vietnamese American pop star Lynda Trang Dai.
This place is locals' favorite that makes great
Vietnamese Sandwiches. Menu favorites include: Xa
Xiu (BBQ Pork) and Shredded Chicken Sandwiches.

THE MARINE ROOM
2000 Spindrift Dr, La Jolla, 858-459-7222
www.marineroom.com
CUISINE: French/Seafood
DRINKS: Full bar
SERVING: Dinner
PRICE RANGE: $$$$

NEIGHBORHOOD: La Jolla Shores
Chic eatery that offers unique opportunity to sit by windows with waves crashing outside at high tide. Creative menu of seafood and French fare. Menu favorites: Black Angus Filet Mignon and Lobster Tail. Nice selection of wines. Fine dining with a beautiful sunset on the shore of La Jolla.

MARKET RESTAURANT & BAR
3702 Via De La Valle, Del Mar, 858-523-0007
www.marketdelmar.com
CUISINE: American (New)
DRINKS: Full bar
SERVING: Lunch/Dinner/Late Night
PRICE RANGE: $$$$
Upscale eatery offering a menu of creative California fare. Menu picks: Flash Seared Local Bluefin Tuna & Crispy Calamari and Coriander-Citrus Glazed

Salmon. Fine dining – great for a special occasion. They rely on the offerings of local farms, including Chino Farm, which is recommended by the famed Alice Waters. Upscale bar scene.

MENYA ULTRA
8199 Clairemont Mesa Blvd, San Diego, 858-571-2010
http://menya-ultra.com
CUISINE: Ramen/Noodles
DRINKS: Beer & Wine
SERVING: Lunch & Dinner
PRICE RANGE: $$
NEIGHBORHOOD: Kearny Mesa
Intimate Ramen eatery offering fresh noodles daily (no MSG here). The bowls here have been called masterful, and after you try one, you'll see why.

Favorites: Nagoya style karaage (Chicken) and Ajitama Ramen. Japanese beer. No reservations.

MESS HALL
In Liberty Public Market
2820 Historic Decatur Rd, San Diego, 714-942-0932
https://bluebridgehospitality.com/libertypublicmarket/
artisan/mess-hall-bar/
CUISINE: American (New)
DRINKS: Full Bar
SERVING: Lunch & Dinner, Breakfast on Sat & Sun
PRICE RANGE: $$$
NEIGHBORHOOD: Liberty Station, Loma Portal,
Point Loma
Located in Liberty Public Market (which features 20 artisan vendors and local famers) so you can order from a variety of venues. Spacious and airy. Most people come here for the cocktails and the laid-back ambiance but there is a simple seasonal menu, which is built around ingredients obtained from other stalls in this market. Clever, yes? Favorites: Duck confit and Polenta.

MISION 19
Mision San Javier 10643, Tijuana, Baja California, 52 664 634 2493
www.mision19.com
CUISINE: Mexican
DRINKS: Full Bar
SERVING: Lunch & Dinner, closed Sun
PRICE RANGE: $$$
NEIGHBORHOOD: Tijuana

Located just five minutes over the border in restaurant
row, this popular Mexican eatery offers an impressive
menu (all in Spanish). There's a chef tasting menu
that features six entrees. Menu favorites include:
Grilled Octopus and Mushroom risotto.
Great selection of cocktails. Worth the trip.

NINE-TEN
910 Prospect St, La Jolla, 858-964-5400
www.nine-ten.com
CUISINE: American
DRINKS: Full Bar
SERVING: Breakfast, Lunch & Dinner
PRICE RANGE: $$$
NEIGHBORHOOD: La Jolla
Located in the **Grande Colonial Hotel**, this casual
eatery offers a menu of classic American fare but
with some twists courtesy of the chef's Jamaican

background. His jerk pork belly dish has plantains, blackeyed peas and a spicy jam-relish. Menu favorites include: Lobster Ravioli and Short Ribs.

NOBU
Located in Hard Rock Hotel San Diego
207 5th Ave (b/t K St & L St), San Diego, 619-814-4124
www.noburestaurants.com
CUISINE: Asian Fusion/Japanese/Sushi
DRINKS: Full Bar
SERVING: Dinner
PRICE RANGE: $$$$
NEIGHBORHOOD: Gaslamp Quarter
The NOBU chain has a high standard and this location lives up to it in every way. Great cocktails and food. You can actually cook your own steak over a hot flaming rock. Cold dishes like Yellowtail

Sashimi and Salmon Tataki are top notch. Make sure you have a reservation.

PIZZA PORT
1956 Bacon St (between Santa Monica & Saratoga Ave), San Diego, 619-224-4700
www.pizzaport.com
CUISINE: Pizza
DRINKS: Beer & Wine Only
SERVING: Lunch & Dinner
PRICE RANGE: $$
NEIGHBORHOOD: Ocean Beach/Point Loma
This local pizza chain is popular with everybody from surfers to families to local businessmen. You eat at large picnic tables in a large, open space. They're known for a variety of pizzas and craft brews. Menu favorites include: Monterey Pizza and Spicy Baked Chicken Wings.

PUESTO

789 W Harbor Dr, San Diego, 619-233-8880
www.eatpuesto.com
CUISINE: Mexican
DRINKS: Full bar
SERVING: Lunch/Dinner
PRICE RANGE: $$
NEIGHBORHOOD: b/t Broadway & Kettner Blvd
Popular two-level restaurant that offers a creative
menu of Mexican fare. Great gourmet tacos and
endless chips and salsa. Vegetarian options. Patio
seating available.

QUAN HY RESTAURANT

9727 Bolsa Ave (between Brookhurst & Bushard St),
Westminster, 714-775-7179
www.quanhyvietnamese.com
CUISINE: Vietnamese

DRINKS: No Booze
SERVING: Lunch & Dinner
PRICE RANGE: $
NEIGHBORHOOD: Westminster
This eatery specializes in Northern Central
Vietnamese cuisine. Banh Beo (Vietnamese steamed
rice discs topped with shrimp) is the signature dish
here. Menu favorites include: Roti Chicken with rice.

ROMESCO BAJA MED BISTRO
4346 Bonita Rd (between Villas Dr & Otay Lakes
Rd), Bonita, 619-475-8627
www.romescomexmed.com
CUISINE: Mexican, Mediterranean
DRINKS: Full Bar
SERVING: Lunch & Dinner, open daily
PRICE RANGE: $$
NEIGHBORHOOD: Chula Vista
Don't let the unusual name throw you—this is some
of the best food in San Diego, because the chef comes
from the other side of the border. This Mediterranean-
Mexican fusion restaurant offers a small plate menu.
Menu favorites include: Tacos Dorados de Cachete
(beef cheek tacos) and Paella (entrée size). Nice
creative cocktails.

ROSE WINE BAR

2219 30th St, San Diego, 619-281-0718
https://www.therosewinebar.com
CUISINE: Wine Bar/American (New)
DRINKS: Full Bar
SERVING: Lunch & Dinner
PRICE RANGE: $$
NEIGHBORHOOD: Ivy St & Juniper St, South Park,
Golden Hill
Neighborhood hangout offering an impressive menu
of natural wines. They've expanded to open a bakery
next door definitely worth checking out. Favorites:
Mushroom Fettuccine and Empanadas. Fresh oysters.
Vegetarian options.

SALUD!

2196 Logan Ave (b/t Sampson St & Evans St), San
Diego, 619-255-3856

https://saludtacos.com/
CUISINE: Mexican
DRINKS: Beer & Wine
SERVING: Breakfast, Lunch, & Dinner
PRICE RANGE: $
NEIGHBORHOOD: Barrio Logan
Hip eatery offers upscale Mexican fare. Daily specials. Beer & salsa bar. Favorites: Grilled shrimp tacos, fire-roasted corn and authentic handmade tortillas. Multiple TVs play old school films.

SOICHI
2121 Adams Ave, San Diego, 619-677-2220
https://www.soichisushi.com
CUISINE: Sushi/Japanese
DRINKS: Beer & Wine
SERVING: Dinner; Closed Mon & Tues
PRICE RANGE: $$$$

NEIGHBORHOOD: Panorama Dr & Mississippi St, University Heights

Upscale Japanese eatery serving traditional dishes, sushi, and sashimi. Also offers a multi-course omakase experience. Michelin rated. Favorites: Chilean Sea Bass and Scallop Nigiri. Tasting menu and a la carte options. Outdoor seating. Reservations recommended.

SOUTH BEACH BAR & GRILLE

5059 Newport Ave (between Bacon St & Abbott St), San Diego, 619-226-4577
www.southbeachob.com
CUISINE: Seafood, Mexican
DRINKS: Full Bar
SERVING: Lunch & Dinner
PRICE RANGE: $$
NEIGHBORHOOD: Ocean Beach

Located right on the pier at the beach, this popular spot features a menu of seafood-focused Mexican cuisine. If it gets packed, just take a table. Also, if you sit upstairs, you'll get one of the best sunset views in the country. Menu favorites include: Mahi grilled fish taco and Lobster Tostadas. The bar offers an impressive selection of microbrews.

STAKE
1309 Orange Ave (b/t Loma Ave & Churchill Pl), Coronado, 619-522-0077
www.stakechophouse.com
CUISINE: Steakhouse/Seafood
DRINKS: Full Bar
SERVING: Dinner
PRICE RANGE: $$$$
NEIGHBORHOOD: Coronado
Old-school steakhouse that is a meat lovers' paradise. I'd say it's the best steakhouse in the area. Filets, chops, pork belly and even seafood dishes. Filet mignon tartar is perfect. Nice wine list.

STARLITE
3175 India St, San Diego, 619-358-9766
www.starlitesandiego.com
CUISINE: Gastropub
DRINKS: Full bar
SERVING: Dinner
PRICE RANGE: $$
NEIGHBORHOOD: Middletown/Mission Hills
Stylish restaurant with menu of creative American fare. This place got the "craft" cocktail craze going in San Diego. Kitchen serves late. Menu picks: Broccoli

and Cheddar Fritters and Grilled Octopus. Crafted cocktails. Patio dining available.

STONE BREWING WORLD BISTRO & GARDENS

2816 Historic Decatur Rd #116, San Diego, 619-269-2100

www.stonebrewing.com/visit/bistros/liberty-station

CUISINE: Gastropub

DRINKS: Beer & Wine Only

SERVING: Lunch & Dinner

PRICE RANGE: $$

NEIGHBORHOOD: Liberty Station

This hip gastropub & brewery offers a creative menu with international eats and craft beers. Menu favorites include: Duck tacos and Wild Boar Sandwich. Bar menu features 40 craft beers on tap and more than 100 bottles. The venue features an outdoor cinema space, a bocce ball court and lush garden.

SUSHI OTA

4529 Mission Bay Dr, San Diego, 858-270-5670
www.sushiota.com
CUISINE: Sushi/Japanese
DRINKS: Beer & Wine
SERVING: Lunch/Dinner, Dinner only on Sat, Sun &
Mon
PRICE RANGE: $$$
NEIGHBORHOOD: Pacific Beach
Located in the corner of a depressing strip mall, but
the menu is top-notch. They serve premium sushi and
omakase tastings. Everything is good here from the
salmon to the octopus.

SUSHI TADOKORO

2244 San Diego Ave, San Diego, 619-297-0298
www.sushitadokoro.com
CUISINE: Sushi Bar/Japanese
DRINKS: Beer & Wine
SERVING: Lunch/Dinner; closed Sun - Tues
PRICE RANGE: $$$
NEIGHBORHOOD: Old Town
Small venue (just 2 dozen seats in a little strip mall)
offering a menu of traditional sashimi and nigiri. One
of the highest rated sushi restaurants in the area. Try
the chef's special. The quality of the fish here is
almost beyond compare. Reservations necessary
unless you want to wait.

TENDER GREENS

4545 La Jolla Village Dr, San Diego, 858-455-9395
www.tendergreens.com
CUISINE: American (New)
DRINKS: Beer & Wine
SERVING: Lunch/Dinner
PRICE RANGE: $$
NEIGHBORHOOD: University City
This place offers an upgraded home-style buffet – pay
at the front and wait for your number to be called.
Creative menu selection. Favorite: Kale salad with
chicken. Interesting sides like roasted squash and
zucchini, roasted eggplant and chickpea salad. Line at
the door moves quickly.

TIGER!TIGER!

3025 El Cajon Blvd, San Diego, 619-487-0401
www.tigertigertavern.blogspot.com/
CUISINE: Sandwiches/Bar Grub
DRINKS: Beer & Wine
SERVING: Dinner, Lunch & Dinner Fri – Sun;
closed Mon
PRICE RANGE: $$
NEIGHBORHOOD: North Park
Casual eatery offering a menu of creative eats like
wood-fired sandwiches. Laid back place wither you
order, grab a number and find a seat – communal
tables. Board games available to keep you occupied
while you wait. Nice pasta selection and beer
selection. Sundays offers a brunch menu only.

TITA'S KITCHENETTE
2720 E Plaza Blvd (at Euclid Ave), National City,
619-434-3879
E Plaza Blvd
CUISINE: Filipino
DRINKS: No Booze
SERVING: Breakfast, Lunch & Dinner
PRICE RANGE: $
NEIGHBORHOOD: National City
This popular Filipino eatery (owned by the same
family for many years) features a revolving menu but
always offers dishes like Pancit, Lumpia, and Pork or
Chicken Adobo. If they offer sweet potato & shrimp
fritters the day you're there, I insist you try them.
They'll usually carry 20 to 25 items on the ever-
changing menu at any one time. You grab a tray and
shuffle down the cafeteria line the way you did when
you were in school. But everything is fresh, fresh,
fresh, not like some buffets where everything is old

the minute they bring it out. Menu favorites include the Chicken teriyaki with beef caldereta. (The grilled meats are the best.) You'll get so much as you pass down the line that you'll end up taking something home. Note: they open at the ungodly hour of 6 A.M., so swing in here for a breakfast like none you've ever had.

TJ OYSTER BAR
4246 Bonita Rd, Bonita, 619-267-4577
Has 3 locations
www.tjoyster.com
CUISINE: Mexican/Seafood
DRINKS: Beer & Wine Only
SERVING: Lunch & Dinner
PRICE RANGE: $
Casual eatery with a nice combo menu featuring both seafood and Mexican fare. Great selection of tacos,

emphasizing fish: my favorites are the garlic shrimp tacos followed by the marlin tacos.

TRIBUTE PIZZA
3077 North Park Way, San Diego, 619-450-4505
https://www.tributepizza.com
CUISINE: Pizza
DRINKS: Full Bar
SERVING: Dinner; Closed Mon & Tues
PRICE RANGE: $$
NEIGHBORHOOD: North Park
Modern pizza eatery serving wood-fired pies smade with fresh ingredients. Lots of vegetarian options. Daily specials. Reservations are strongly encouraged.

TRUST RESTAURANT
3752 Park Blvd, San Diego, 619-795-6901
https://www.trustrestaurantsd.com
CUISINE: American (New)
DRINKS: Full Bar
SERVING: Dinner; Closed Mon & Tues
PRICE RANGE: $$
NEIGHBORHOOD: Robinson Ave & Essex St.
Hillcrest
Beautifully decorated modern eatery offering a
seasonal menu of New American cuisine. Favorites:
Albacore Tartare and Smoke Braised Lamb.

Vegetarian options. Creative cocktails. Indoor/outdoor seating. Separate bar area.

TURF SUPPER CLUB
1116 25th St (b/t C St & B St), San Diego, 619-234-6363
www.turfsupperclub.com
CUISINE: Steakhouse
DRINKS: Full Bar
SERVING: Dinner, Lunch & Dinner Fri - Sun
PRICE RANGE: $$
NEIGHBORHOOD: Golden Hill
Unique dining experience where you get to grill your own steak. I found the whole experience a little off-putting. (Why wouldn't I stay home if I wanted to cook the meal?) Favorites: Marinated flank steak and top sirloin. Over 21 crowd who come for the retro cocktail lounge. NOTE: Go with someone who knows how to cook because dinner is in their hands.

UNDERBELLY

750 W Fir St (at Kettner Blvd), San Diego, 619-269-4626

www.godblessunderbelly.com
CUISINE: Japanese
DRINKS: Beer & Wine Only
SERVING: Lunch & Dinner
PRICE RANGE: $$
NEIGHBORHOOD: Little Italy
If you're a fan of classic Japanese cuisine, then you'll become a fan of this unpretentious open-air ramen noodle counter right in the middle of Little Italy. A nice feature is that they offer over 20 beers on tap and about half of these are from local breweries in what has become beer-crazy San Diego. The Pork Belly Bao buns are delicious but the signature dish is the "Belly of the Beast," which is fully loaded with all the fixins.

VILLA SAVERIOS

Escuadron 201 s/n, 22420 Tijuana, Baja California, +52 664 686 6442

www.villasaverios.com
CUISINE: Italian
DRINKS: Full Bar
SERVING: Lunch & Dinner
PRICE RANGE: $$$
NEIGHBORHOOD: Tijuana
Take a trip across the border for this lovely fine-dining Italian eatery with dishes prepared with a distinct Mexican flair. Menu favorites include:

Barbocoa Crispy Tacos and Yellow Tuna. Nice wine selection.

WAYFARER BREAD & PASTRY
5525 La Jolla Blvd, (b/t Forward St & Midway St), San Diego, 858-454-1924
www.wayfarerbread.com
CUISINE: Bakery
DRINKS: No Booze
SERVING: Breakfast & Lunch
PRICE RANGE: $$
NEIGHBORHOOD: La Jolla – Bird Rock
Popular local bakery offering the best croissants ever (one version had strawberry jam and pistachio butter). You'll leave with a bag full. Nice selection of scones, cinnamon rolls, and other baked goods. Butter-brushed sourdough bread is excellent.

WINE VAULT & BISTRO

3731 India St, San Diego, 619-295-3939
www.winevaultbistro.com
CUISINE: American (New)/Wine Bar
DRINKS: Full bar
SERVING: Lunch/Dinner/Late Night
PRICE RANGE: $$
NEIGHBORHOOD: Middletown/Mission Hills
Charming eatery offering a menu of eclectic fare.
Fixed-price menu that's VERY reasonable.
Communal tables. Great wine pairings. Menu changes
often.
Charming spot offers eclectic fare, wine flights & a
fixed-price menu served at communal tables.

Pork belly at Wrench

WRENCH AND RODENT

1815 S Coast Hwy, Oceanside, 760-271-0531
https://www.seabasstropub.com
CUISINE: Sushi/American (New)
DRINKS: Beer & Wine
SERVING: Dinner; Mon & Tues
PRICE RANGE: $$
NEIGHBORHOOD: Kelly St & Cassidy St /
Oceanside
Popular eatery offering a varied menu of sushi,
sashimi, and New American fare. Known for their
fresh local fish and produce. Favorites: Seared
Albacore and Seared Swordfish Nigiri. Vegan
options.

YAKITORI TAISHO

5185 Clairemont Mesa Blvd, San Diego, 858-752-0468

http://sandiegoyakyudori.com/page/taisho

CUISINE: Japanese

DRINKS: Beer & Wine

SERVING: Dinner; closed Thurs. & Sun

PRICE RANGE: $$

NEIGHBORHOOD: Clairemont

Intimate eatery offering a creative Japanese menu. Known for yakitori, with items like grilled chicken skin, chicken meatballs and chicken wings deconstructed. Come early and expect a wait. Unique concept of ordering but the food is worth it.

FOOD MARKETS

CHINO FARM

6123 Calzada Del Bosque, Rancho Santa Fe, 858-756-3184

www.chinofamilyfarm.com

In the fertile hills a few miles east of Solana Beach, you'll find the roadside headquarters of Chino Farms, a Japanese American family operation that produces fruit and vegetables beloved by chefs such as Alice Waters and Wolfgang Puck. The stand, officially known as the Vegetable Shop, has been in business since 1969.

LITTLE ITALY MERCATO

600 W Date St, San Diego, 619-233-3901
www.littleitalymercato.com
NEIGHBORHOOD: Little Italy
Saturday market with over 150 vendors offering fresh produce, meat, eggs, crafts, plants, prepared foods, pastries, art, and much more. Great spot for breakfast. Many of the vendors offer free samples. Live music.

BREWERIES

San Diego is a lot more than surf, sand and sex on the
beach. To fuel all this activity, a brewery explosion
has been going on. There are some 50 breweries in
the county and the number seems to grow every year.

There's even something called **San Diego Beer
Week**, an event occurring every November, that
celebrates "all things beer" in San Diego.

www.sdbeer.com/

More urgently, there's even a **TapHunter ap** that'll
tell you the brands on tap at local bars and
restaurants.

Sounds exhausting, doesn't it?

Take a bus tour of breweries, if you like. They have them. Try:

BREWERY TOURS OF SAN DIEGO
www.brewerytoursofsandiego.com

If you want to shop for some hard-to-find bottled beer, try out:

BOTTLECRAFT BEER SHOP & TASTING ROOM
2161 India St., San Diego, 619-487-9493
www.bottlecraftbeer.com
Here's a very short list of breweries I especially liked when I visited last. I'll add more in the next edition when I update it in a few months.

ALESMITH BREWING CO
9990 AleSmith Ct, San Diego, 858-549-9888

www.alesmith.com
An artisanal microbrewery featuring a rotating draft menu, a tasting room and free tours. Very popular and the tasting room is usually packed.

BALLAST POINT
9045 Carroll Way, San Diego, 858-790-6900
www.ballastpoint.com
Great brewery with a high-end restaurant attached that offers a creative menu of delicious treats like Caramelized Foie Gras Custard and Caramelized Onion and Brie Flatbread. Reservations recommended. Enormous beer selection, free brewery tours – sign up bcforc you eat so you won't have to wait.

CULTURE BREWING CO
111 S Cedros Ave Suite 200, Solana Beach, 858-345-1144
www.culturebrewingco.com
Trendy microbrewery with a tasting room featuring a large selection of craft beers on tap. Nice tour. Patio seating.

HESS BREWING CO
3812 Grim Ave, San Diego, 619-255-7136
www.mikehessbrewing.com
One of the premier craft breweries in San Diego. This is the city's first production nono-brewery and its 33rd brewery, it upholds a reputation for great beers. Unique brewery and tasting room experience. Variety of beers and brews offered for tasting.

KARL STRAUSS BREWING COMPANY
1157 Columbia St, San Diego, 619-234-2739
www.karlstrauss.com
Popular brewing company and large facility. Nice selection of pints and beer pretzels.

SOCIETE BREWING COMPANY
8262 Clairemont Mesa Blvd, San Diego, 858-598-5409
www.societebrewing.com
Large brewery and tasting room that specializes in Belgian-style and barrel-aged beer. The tasting room offers 14 house brews on tap. Large communal tables. Sometimes there are food trucks.

WHITE LABS
9495 Candida St, San Diego, 858-693-3441
www.whitelabs.com
Popular tasting room with a regularly rotating list of beers – all created on-site. The yeast for their beer is sold worldwide.
This tasting room features a regularly changing line-up of beers created on-site.
A unique brewery because their main product is not the beer, but the yeast which is sold worldwide.
Interesting tour as the brewery is more like a lab. No photos allowed.

INDEX

www.ingramcontent.com/pod-product-compliance
Ingram Content Group UK Ltd.
Pitfield, Milton Keynes, MK11 3LW, UK
UKHW021646190726
13853UKWH00001B/81